G000152698

5

QUICK STEPS TO BECOMING

A MUSIC PRODUCER

Elvine Robert

While every precaution has been taken in the preparation of this book, the publisher assumes no responsibility for errors or omissions, or damages resulting from the use of the information contained herein.

5 Quick Steps to Becoming a Music Producer

Second edition. January 6, 2020.

Contents

About the Author

Elvine Robert is a passionate music lover who has committed himself for years now to assisting music lovers around the world. This he does on social media platforms, with his books, etc. His area of specialty is narrowed down to singing, playing the piano, and music production.

Although Elvine started as a singer in the church choir, he went on to become a pianist and a music producer, which lead him to be of great value to his choir and others around him.

INTRODUCTION

Hi, I am Elvine Robert, and I will be taking you through 5 quick steps to becoming a music producer.

In my journey to becoming a music producer, I passed through a lot of hurdles, of which a majority originated from not knowing the next step to take or skipping some essential steps, which lead to a slow learning and development process. As a result of this, I decided to write this book to give a clear step by step guide to becoming a good music producer. This book will be covering *5 quick steps to becoming a music producer* as well as giving you the foundation (of which you would build on) to becoming a good music producer.

There are other hurdles you may have to scale through, which would be a fun journey with the right motivation and willpower. By carefully reading this book, you should have a vivid understanding of music production and how to go about becoming a good music producer.

STEP 1: Get the Basic Tools Needed for Music Production

Before anyone can go into the production of anything, you would agree with me that such a person would need some basic kind of working tools. In music production, these are the tools you would need to be able to produce good music. I have categorized these working tools into hardware and software tools.

Hardware Tools

I will be taking you through the hardware tools or materials you must have for you to be able to produce good music. I will be giving each of these hardware tools a rating of **1 to 5 stars** based on how relevant they are for you to **start producing music**. We will be looking at three hardware tools:

1. A personal computer

Having a personal computer (PC) is the most basic must-have for you to start your voyage as a music producer. This is the interface that connects with the other hardware and where your chosen Digital Audio Workstation (DAW) is installed. It is like the brain of the entire music production operation. A PC (which could be a laptop or a desktop) is a must-have and would be rated **5 stars**.

2. Monitor speakers and headphones

To be able to listen to the music you are creating, knowing if it sounds the way you have imagined, you would need a good pair of monitor speakers and headphones.

A good pair of monitor speakers is necessary for listening and adjusting the low frequency of your music; to know if the bass and kick and other low ends are sounding the way you want them to, while a pair of monitor headphones are ideally used for listening to the mid-range and the high frequency of your music. You should note that a pair of monitor headphones are different from the usual headphones like "Beats by Dre" because they are not enhanced in their bass region or in anything, such that they sound flat, and you can make your music sound as it would in your laptop, car, etc.

You could also make use of a pair of iPhone headphones, not because they are the best headphones when compared with others, but because they are what a majority of the world's population use in listening to music. So, if your music does not sound good on a pair of iPhone headphones, then your music may not be liked very much.

I will be giving you a list of monitor speakers and headphones you should consider buying on

Amazon or any other platform of your choice. You should also do a little research on monitor speakers and headphones so that you can be sure of the quality of what you are buying.

Monitor speakers to consider buying: FOSTEX PMO.4D, KRK ROCKIT 5, ADAM F5, YAMAHA HS7, PIONEER SDJ80X, and PRESONUS ERIS 4.5 2 WAY POWERED STUDIO MONITOR. For cheaper monitor speakers with excellent sound, you should consider MACKIE CR3 or M-AUDIO AV-42.

Monitor headphones to consider buying: BAYERDYNAMIC DT 770 PRO-80, AUDIO TECHNICA ATH-M50X, BAYERDYNAMIC DT 880 PRO, SONY MDR-7506, and KRK KNS 8400. For cheaper monitor headphones, you should consider SONY MDRV6 or IPHONE HEADPHONES.

Based on how relevant a pair of monitor speakers and a pair of headphones are for you to kick off your musical voyage, I will be rating both separately. A pair of monitor headphones are a must-have and would be rated **5 stars,** and a pair of monitor speakers is something every producer should have and would be rated **4 stars**.

3. Midi keyboard

If you are looking for what would take your music production to the next level, then having a midi keyboard will do just that. Having a midi keyboard is not something you should think of getting, but something you should have to move to the next level in music production.

A midi keyboard makes arranging your sound easier in your chosen DAW (will come to this later). What this does is that it allows you to play whatever melody or chord you want to play directly into your chosen DAW. For example, if your chosen DAW is FL studio, instead of you trying to figure out the timing of the chords or melody you want to play and arranging all this in the piano roll, you just play them in using a midi keyboard, and it records them right into the piano roll of FL studio. So with this, you can get more creative with your music. I will be giving the midi keyboard a rating of **3 stars** because you do not need it to start music production.

A midi keyboard you should consider buying is M-AUDIO KEYSTATION. You could also do a little research.

Software Tools

These are the tools you would be installing in your PC to produce music. We have the DAW, the VST plugins, and high-quality samples. I will be rating these software tools from **1 to 5 stars** based on how relevant these tools are to start producing music.

1. Digital audio workstation (DAW)

This is a software program that is installed on your PC, and it is where all the music creation is done. It is the place where you create your drum beat, chord progressions for your piano, and any other instrument you wish to add to your music creation. Different types of DAWs do virtually the same thing and these are <u>IMAGE LINE FL STUDIO</u>[1], <u>APPLE LOGIC PRO</u>[2], <u>STEINBERG CUBASE</u>[3], and <u>ABLETON LIVE</u>[4]. These are only but a few. There are many other DAWs out there, of which the ones mentioned above are the most common. Having a DAW is as essential as having a PC. So, it would be rated **5 stars**.

2. VST plug-in and high-quality samples

Virtual Studio Technology (VST) plug-ins are software tools that are installed and linked with your chosen DAW to produce sounds that simulate traditional recording studio hardware in software. What this does is that it simulates your traditional piano, guitar, bass, violin, or any other instruments into a software version such that you would be able to play these instruments without using these traditional instruments. Examples of VST plug-ins

---

[1] https://www.image-line.com/flstudio/

[2] https://www.apple.com/lae/logic-pro/

[3] https://www.steinberg.net/en/products/cubase/cubase_pro.html

[4] https://www.ableton.com/en/trial/

are **Sylenth**[5], **Serum**[6], **Massive**[7], and **Spire**[8]. Others are **Omnisphere**[9], **Kontakt**[10], **and Nexus**[11], etc.

High-quality samples are sounds that could be from an instrument or vocalist. These samples cover different kinds of kicks, snares, open-hat, hi-hat, some vocal sounds, instrumental sounds, etc. You can get high-quality samples from **Splice sound**[12]. Having a VST plug-in or having high-quality samples will improve your music creations, but since most DAW comes with their plug-ins or sounds, you can decide to work with them until you have gotten familiar with your DAW and wish to take your musical career to the next level. For this

---

[5] https://www.lennardigital.com/sylenth1/

[6] https://www.xferrecords.com/products/serum

[7] https://www.native-instruments.com/en/products/komplete/synths/massive/

[8] https://www.reveal-sound.com/index.html

[9] https://www.spectrasonics.net/products/omnisphere/

[10] https://www.native-instruments.com/en/products/komplete/samplers/kontakt-5/

[11] https://refx.com/nexus/

[12] https://splice.com/features/sounds

reason, VST plug-ins and high-quality samples would be rated **3 stars.**

To set yourself in the right direction, you may need to book a session with a studio to get a clearer understanding of the hardware and software tools you need for your journey as a music producer. If you're lucky enough, you might find a local sound engineer who will let you sit in for a while to have an experience of the tools that make their music sound top-notch.

Now, you don't need to know how to play various instruments but what you may need to know is how all these pieces of equipment come together. You may need to know how to set your microphone, how to arrange your monitor speakers for optimal effect, and how everything comes together.

You Don't Need Expensive Equipment to Sound Good

So many musicians are looking for things that will make them better in their music voyage. And without so much thinking about, they put in so much effort trying to get the most expensive equipment to stand out from the crowd. Perhaps they believe it will help them sound better and be more creative. Yes, of course, it can. Using high-quality gears and equipment can be quite a game-changer. However, it gets to a point where money can no longer improve the results these musicians want. We'll be looking at some reasons why.

Talent and hard work

Yes, money can buy a lot of things and can even make you look like a good music producer, but this doesn't mean that you'd end up being creative like one. Our minds have been tricked into believing that what we need to be better is that perfect midi keyboard, guitar, or DAW setup. It is as though these things are what is standing on our way and preventing us from making the ideal and beautiful music we hope to create, but this isn't true.

What makes one a good music producer is hard work and sometimes, talent, or maybe both. Spending numerous amounts of time in the studio, practicing, and experimenting is the best play to becoming an outstanding music producer and not necessarily the expensive equipment you use. Now, having the most expensive kit can be quite helpful, but without the right creative power behind them, they become nothing more but overpriced accessories.

Creativity

Poorly made and cheap musical instruments constitute a serious challenge today, mainly for those who are in the beginning stage of their musical journey. However, it gets to the sweet point where the price level is just enough to give the needed quality of equipment such that most musical ideas and creativity can be voiced through them. It doesn't matter if you're trying to create a beautiful beat or trying to improve on your creativity, moderately priced equipment is most times all you need to get the job done.

It can be inspiring and exhilarating to make use of expensive gears and instruments, but these are not prerequisites for becoming an outstanding and credible music producer. Indeed, many of the great musicians we've heard and still hearing of today didn't start with expensive equipment but instead became outstanding while making use of moderately priced equipment or even cheap and poorly made ones.

So, like how expensive music gears and instruments don't make you an outstanding music producer so also moderately priced music equipment doesn't make you a bad one.

Goals

At times purchasing hefty gears and instruments can make you feel like you are closer to your goals and aspirations. But in reality, everything we acquire will be of no value to us if we don't know how to use them appropriately.

Music can be a lot of work, and progress can, at times, be slow. So we might be tempted to associate the shiny new stuff we buy with growth and improvement. However, these two things are separate from each other. Once the celebratory aspect of buying new things is over, you'll be faced with the same old challenges you had while using modestly priced equipment.

Now, you can choose to use expensive and luxurious equipment if you can afford them, there is nothing wrong with that. However, when you keep hoping that getting the right headphones, monitor speakers, or microphone will make you become the music producer you've always aspired to be, then

5 Quick Steps to Becoming a Music Producer

you'll be better off making do with what you have and putting in the needed work.

STEP 2: Get to Know the Basics of Music Theory

To be a good music producer; you would have to know music theory. The more knowledgeable you are in music theory, the more creative you would be when it comes to music production. In fact, you are likely to be a better music producer if you can play a musical instrument.

What You Should Know in Music Theory

I will be giving you a guide on what you should know in music theory to improve your creativity as a music producer. These would be generally classified under **Melody** and **Harmony**.

Melody

When it comes to melody, you should know what a musical scale is, what a melody is, and how you can make use of them. Let me give a brief explanation.

What is a musical scale?

In music theory, a scale is any set of musical notes that are arranged according to their pitch. When arranged according to an increase in pitch, it is called an ascending scale, and when ordered according to a decrease in pitch, it is called a descending scale.

Now, we have the two most common scales in music, which are the major and minor scales. The major scale is something we are familiar with and it is audibly voiced as, doh-re-me-fah-so-la-ti-do. What is a melody?

A melody is when these scales are played in different orders and patterns to produce a unique sound.

Harmony

Under harmony, you should know what chords are, how they are structured, what chord progressions are, and the principles that govern these chord progressions.

What is a chord?

A chord is a combination of notes which, when played together, blends harmonically. Now, these combinations can be three, four, five, six, and seven notes.

When it comes to the structure of chords, we are talking about the intervals between each note in a chord. We have both melodic and harmonic intervals.

What is a chord progression?

A chord progression is a transition or progress from one chord to the other. These movements are governed by some theories and patterns, one of which is the circle of fifth pattern.

Getting to know music theory will help you to be able to make use of good melody lines, chords, and cool chord progressions that would make your music sound good and professional. You should take a look at one of my books on how to play the piano titled "**Beginner's Guide to Playing the Piano Professionally**[13]."

---

[13] https://www.books2read.com/u/3kreXG

STEP 3: know what Song structure is

What is song structure all about you may ask yourself? Before I can go into that, let me help you understand the importance of knowing the structure of the song you are producing. When you understand the structure of the song you are making, it helps you to know how to arrange your beats, and where you should add a different instrument to the song or where your bass or drums should come in. At the beginning of most songs, when creating the beats, it is important to allow these beats to build up rather than having everything happen all at once. This brings in variations into your music and makes listeners *not to get bored* when listening to your music. Also, having a pre-chorus, a bridge, etc. in your music also have positive effects on your listeners.

Getting to Know About Music Genre

So, to be able to know the structure of a song or music piece you're creating, you'd have to know the genre it falls under. Every music piece falls under a genre or subgenre, and they do as a result of a repetitive pattern. The classification of music into types helps us to understand how music is created from a much clearer perspective, and this makes it easier to recognize patterns, recommend music artists, and also identify the type of music creation we enjoy most.

At the initial stage of my journey as a music producer, I didn't see the importance of music genres. I felt it was a limitation to one's creativity as it streamlined you to a specified pattern and form. However, I later discovered that the classification of music into different genres and subgenres helps to bring clarity, recognition, and appreciation of the creations of music artists. It also makes it possible to be more creative as a music producer.

What is Song Structure?

Since I have somewhat covered some of the benefits of knowing the structure of the song you are creating, I will now lay more emphasis on what song structure is, so you can get a better understanding of the information I am trying to pass across.

Generally, song structure is just the arrangement of your song or how your song is patterned. I will be listing some standard song structures that are used in the majority of the songs we hear today.

Verse/Chorus/Verse/Chorus/Bridge/Chorus: this is also known as the ABABCB structure. Where A, B, and C represent the verse, chorus, and bridge, respectively.

Verse/Pre-Chorus/Chorus/Verse/Pre-Chorus/Chorus/Bridge/Chorus: this is another kind of song structure with a slight variation from the first structure mentioned earlier. If you look closely, you will see that the "pre-chorus" was the only change that was made.

Verse/Verse/Bridge/Verse: this structure is also known as the AABA. In this case, A and B represent verse and bridge, respectively.

From all the above structures, you would agree with me that knowing the song structure or pattern of the music you are creating will help improve your music creativity a great deal.

STEP 4: Get to Know Your Chosen DAW and Learn to Produce Music with it

N ow that you have chosen a DAW, you have to get to know and understand how your DAW works (if you're yet to choose a DAW, I would recommend FL studio as your chosen DAW). This is where you get to know how to navigate through your DAW, like moving from your mixer to your piano roll (where you arrange the notes or chords of your instrument), or anywhere you want to go and how to create beats using the DAW. I recommend watching YouTube videos on how to use your chosen DAW and busyworsksbeats.com[14] to learn more about music production.

I make use of FL STUDIO and CUBASE. It took me a while to even understand how to navigate through the FL STUDIO interface, but with more effort and time, I was able to produce beats that were okay for a beginner, although it didn't sound as professional as I hoped but was good for a start.

To improve on your creativity, try listening to different songs and try to depict and separate the different sounds and effects in these songs. You can devote a few hours to listening to new music each week, and this can help you think about your craft differently and more productively.

To create a top-notch sound is never an easy task. The first things you need are a pair of headphones and a good laptop, and you're good to go. While having these basic tools is necessary to start your voyage as a music producer, you may

---

[14] http://www.busyworksbeats.com/

lack the essential skills required to reach a good level of production. So, having the right tools is good, but in addition to this, you'll need to be able to make use of these tools efficiently.

We'll be looking at some things you can do to help improve your music production skills and also help you learn and grow faster.

Try New Things, Be Adventurous

Putting in the time and effort as a musician or music producer will, in the long run, help improve and make you develop in your craft, that is, if you're consistent. However, there is an aspect of development we rarely look at, and this is the readiness for an artist to explore and be adventurous.

Whether you're just starting or an experienced professional, being able to test and experiment with new things is an indication that you would continue to improve and thus, be successful. We'll be looking at a few things you can try out to break out of your comfort zone and be adventurous.

New Plugins

Most music producers find it challenging to leave their comfort zone to try new things. They most times prefer sticking to what they know. At times the extra creativity we need may be in trying new things and in that process, discovering unique sounds that would help make your current project to stand out.

New Instruments

Having a set of tools and instruments you can get yourself familiar with is essential if you want to translate your musical ideas into songs easily. One way you can get these types of equipment is to look for used instruments online. There are a lot of people who are looking to get rid of their old gears and equipment. So you don't need to spend much to get hold of new gear and instruments.

Allowing yourself to explore new possibilities and new sounds with various plugins and instruments will help bring a fresh perspective to your music creations. Now, getting yourself familiar with new sounds and instruments gives you a more comprehensive range of ideas you can incorporate into your music creation, thus increasing your creativity levels.

Arrangement and Organization

Most music producers overlook the need for organization and arrangement. When you can integrate organization into your music production process, it makes it easier for you to be able to transfer your ideas and imaginations into your chosen DAW in a faster and more effective way, and it also gives room to focus more on the creation process.

Let's look at a few steps and actions you can take to be a more organized music producer.

Plugin arrangement and organization

We've looked at some plugins you can use in music production. Now, to make sure everything goes smoothly and to prevent hiccups, organizing these plugins according to saturators, limiters, reverbs, etc. might be very useful. In situations where you find yourself having to search for a specific plugin during a project can be a creativity killer. So, always try to keep it organize to encourage good workflow.

Sample arrangement and organization

Getting high-quality audio samples can be essential in improving your creative ability. However, if these samples are not organized in an order that makes it easy to navigate through them, then it could be tedious and can inhibit creativity.

If I'm honest, this process is very challenging and time-consuming, but it is the most useful in terms of getting stuff organized. Take the time to arrange your samples by following the type of sound they produce or any other pattern you can find. The more thorough and specific you are in your arrangement, the easier it is to find what you're looking for and, thus, bring your ideas into reality.

Self-Awareness

Being self-conscious and self-aware of your abilities as a music producer can be essential for your success. Are there areas in your music you need to work and improve on? Do you think your music creations are of good quality and standard? Try answering these questions, and be honest with yourself. Don't let your ego be a stumbling block to your music, music career, and in your journey to success. Be self-aware of where you are currently and where you want to be.

Let's look at a few things you can do to become more self-aware.

Compare your music to other artists

Keep in mind that the goal here is not to get discouraged. When you compare your music creations with that of other well-known and reputable music artists, you might discover that their creations are a whole lot better than yours. Now, see it as an opportunity to set a goal for yourself. Try to assure yourself that you can reach your set goal with hard work and lots of practice.

Ask for advice

Asking others for advice can help you see things from a different perspective and can be an eye-opening experience. Look for someone you trust and admire and ask them for their advice and assistance. Preferably, someone that has accomplished a lot in music or a well-trusted friend that is taking the same journey with you. Ask for criticism on your music, or anything else you feel will help you improve in your journey as a music producer.

Ear Training

Every music artist, in one way or the other, has trained their ears to be more sensitive to musical sounds. What I mean by this is not only limited to being able to distinguish between notes, specific intervals, chords, and chords progressions but also to understand the kind of sounds that blends well together in a song. If you can't arrange various textures and timbres of sounds such that they blend perfectly well together, then you have a slim chance of succeeding and becoming what you hope to be.

Let's look at some ways you can develop and train your ears.

Practicing

There are various apps and websites you can make use of to improve your hearing skills. By practicing, you will be able to develop a clear understanding of what is really going on in a music piece. And having this skill will make it possible for you to make better music. Try taking exercises on intervals, scales, chords, and chord progressions.

Take notes

Taking note of the elements that go together in your favorite songs and why they do is a great way to train your ears. Write down the various instruments used, the kind of sounds produced by each of these instruments, how they are arranged in the music piece, how they are mixed, or anything else you feel is essential.

Patience

This is an essential skill to have if you wish to be a successful music producer. If you're not patient with yourself, your music, and your music career, then you will find it challenging to reach your set goals. If you've ever read the success stories of various artists, you'll see that a majority of them put in years and years of hard work into their music career before they got to where they are today. Although, it might seem like it all happened overnight.

Let's look at a few tips that will help increase your patience level.

Taking breaks

Of course, devoting a majority of your time and effort into your craft is essential, but at times, it is good to step back a bit to clear your head from it all. When you work too hard without taking breaks, you might find yourself producing lesser results. You can't become a professional or superstar overnight. It takes time and effort – Rome wasn't built in a day.

Set up goals for yourself

Sometimes it is good to set for yourself long term and short term goals. This will help to push you through challenging times you'd be faced with during your music voyage. Short terms goals will act as motivation to help you push forward towards your long term goals. Having these long terms goals will help make sure that you stay on track and don't go off track.

STEP 5: Understand How to Mix and Master

Here, I will be focusing on how you can mix and master the beats you have created using your chosen DAW. Mixing and mastering are two different things entirely. Mixing is like the making process of artwork, while mastering is the finishing process to make the artwork look its possibly best. With that concept in mind, we will be looking at mixing and mastering separately

What is mixing?

For easy understanding, mixing is the adjusting of the volume and panning level of your multi-track recording. Note that this is not the complete definition of mixing as mixing also deals with the adding of effects such as reverb, delay, etc. to your recordings as well as other mixing plugins such as equalizers, compressors, limiters, etc.

We will be looking at some basic terms used in mixing that you would need to get familiar with to be able to understand what mixing is all about.

Volume

This has to do with the loudness of each track of your recordings. Here you have to adjust the loudness of each track to your taste. For example, if you want the drums to stand out in your recordings (probably because you added a lot of swings to it), you can start by making it the loudest.

Panning

This is basically the spread of the mix. It is about the arrangement of your sounds in each track either to the left, right, or center of your recording. Basically, low ends sounds are usually panned to the left while the high ends to the right, as we can see in our live mic, piano, etc. because this is what our ears are used to. This does not mean that you should always pan your bass guitar to the left and other high ends to the right, you can do whatever your ears tell you to do, but looking at most songs, you would notice that the bass sound is usually left at the center of the stereo field. Leaving all your sounds panned centrally would make your mix sound crowded and flat.

Equalizers/Equalizing

Every sound we hear is made up of frequencies which are measured in Hertz (Hz). Equalizing is the art of removing, enhancing, and trying to balance all the frequencies in your mix to get a better sound.

Think of it as vocals; a male vocalist with a deep voice is at the bottom frequency spectrum, another male vocalist with less bass in his voice is at the mid-range and a high pitched female vocalist at the top.

Just like I have described using vocals, you would notice that the frequency spectrum is described using the Lows, Mids, and Highs. What this means is that a bass instrument or even a kick with a low-heavy and boomy sound would be seen mostly at the lows in the frequency spectrum, while a snare or a hi-hat would be seen at the mids or highs of the frequency spectrum because they are a lot tinier in sound than the bass instrument.

Equalizers are plugins that are used for enhancing or removing frequencies you do not want and do every other thing about equalizing to make your mix sound better. An example of an equalizer is the parametric EQ 2 (an FL studio 12 plug-in).

Compression

This has to do with the taming of the dynamic range of your mix. This is done with a compressor that sets specific limits on how much frequency it is to let through, adjusting the compressor's ratio for how much work the compressor does and the attack and release time to know when the compression starts and stops. What this does is to tame the highest frequency that is loudest and boost the lower and quieter ones.

Reverb

Reverb is an effect that would make your music sound much cooler and interesting. What this does is that it makes your drums, vocals, or any other instrument sound as if they were in a small room, large room, or a large hall, etc. so, you could make your instrument sound differently. For example, you could make your snare drum sound like the kind of "in your face" sound or you could make it sound as if it is a bit far from you by adding reverb to it.

What is Mastering?

This is all about making a mix which sounds good to sound professional. It is taking a mix and adjusting levels to correct mix balance issues, unifying the mix, and maintaining consistency across an album. By maintaining consistency, I mean by making sure that one track is not louder than the other in an album such that listeners would not have to adjust volume when playing your album. Mastering could also involve adding of Equalizers, compressors, and limiters to the mix.

Note: this is only but an introduction to the art of mixing and mastering.

5 Quick Steps to Becoming a Music Producer (Summary)

Step 1: Get a good PC, install your chosen DAW, get a pair of headphones, and you are good to go.

Step 2: learn to play melodies, chords, and chord progressions.

Step 3: know the pattern the genre of the music you are creating follows.

Step 4: understand how your chosen DAW works, create beats with it, and don't stop exploring.

Step 5: understand the concept of mixing and mastering. Mix and master your beats, and you are a music producer.

Printed in Great Britain
by Amazon